Tiny Life in a Puddle

By Bobbi Early

Consultants

Reading Adviser
Nanci Vargus, EdD
Assistant Professor of Literacy
University of Indianapolis
Indianapolis, Indiana

Subject Adviser
Howard A. Shuman, PhD
Department of Microbiology
Columbia University Medical Center
New York, New York

Children's Press®
A Division of Scholastic Inc.
New York Toronto London Auckland Sydney
Mexico City New Delhi Hong Kong
Danbury, Connecticut

Designer: Herman Adler Design
Photo Researcher: Caroline Anderson
The photo on the cover shows algae.

Library of Congress Cataloging-in-Publication Data

Early, Bobbi, 1961–
 Tiny life in a puddle / by Bobbi Early.
   p. cm. — (Rookie read-about science)
  Includes index.
  ISBN 0-516-25272-0 (lib. bdg.)   0-516-25475-8 (pbk.)
 1. Protista—Juvenile literature. 2. Freshwater microbiology—Juvenile
literature. 3. Microscopy—Juvenile literature. I. Title. II. Series.
  QR74.5.E27 2005
  579'.176—dc22   2005004628

Splash in a puddle.
What happens?

You get wet!

Millions of tiny living things live in puddles. These living things are called protists (PROH-tists).

Protists are too small to see.

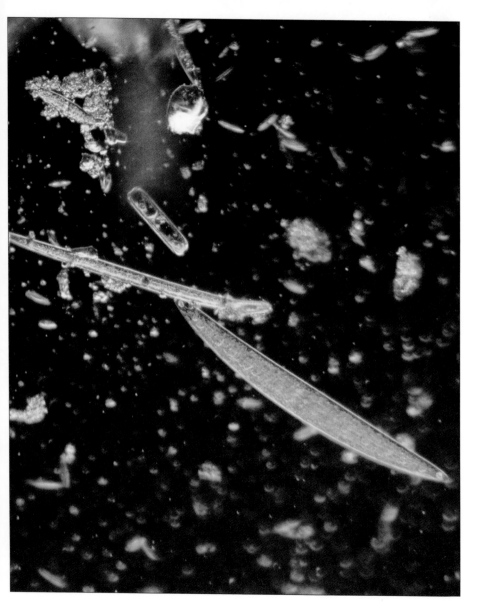

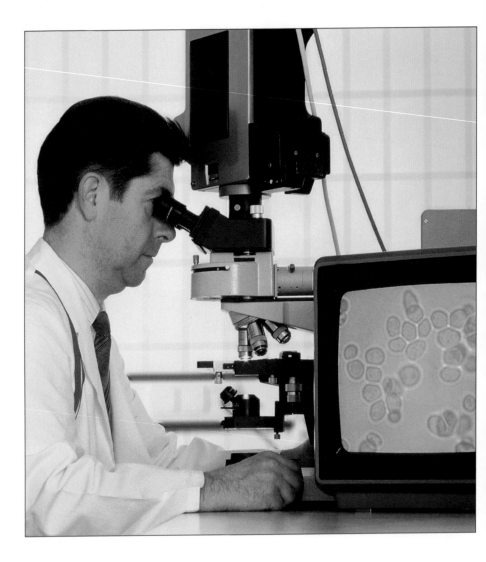

Scientists look through microscopes to study them.

Microscopes make the tiny protists look bigger.

Protists can be many shapes. These protists look like trumpets.

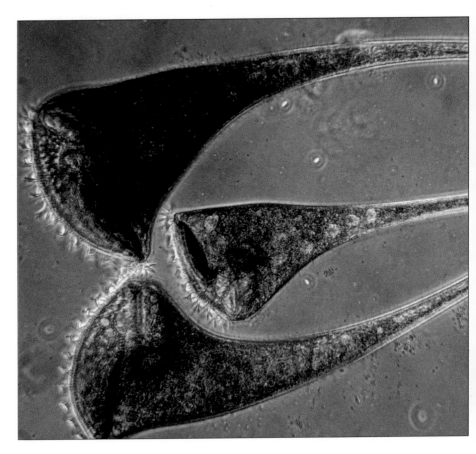

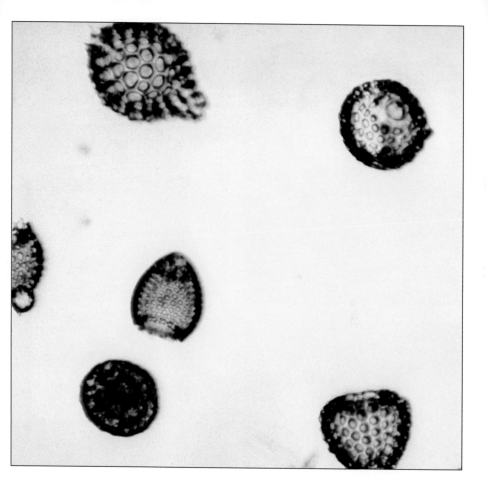

What do you think these protists look like?

10

Some kinds of protists have a special part. This part looks like a thick hair. This part pushes the protist through the water.

This kind of protist is covered with tiny hair-like parts. These parts act like oars. They help move the protist through the puddle.

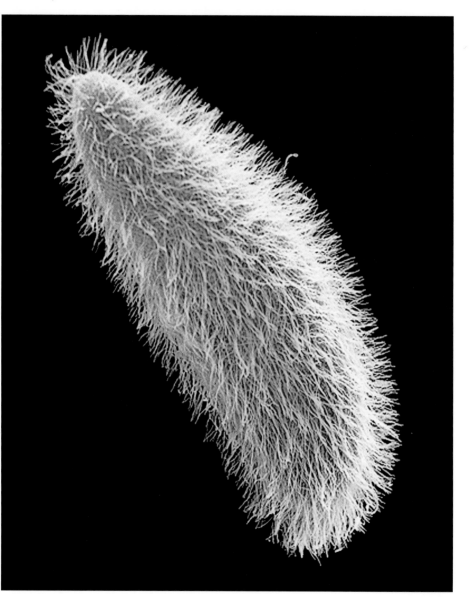

13

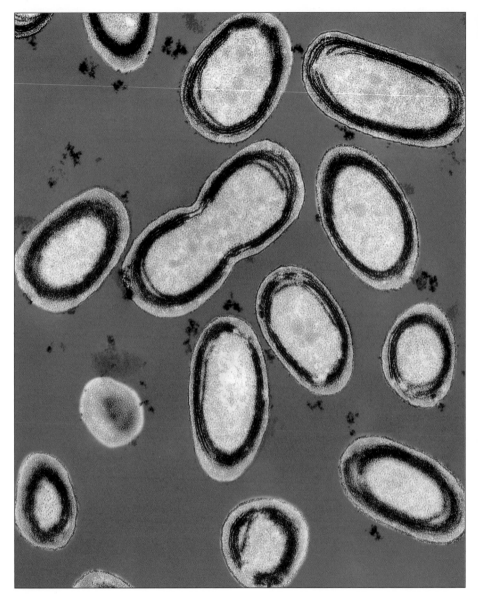

14

Some protists make their own food. They use water and sunlight to make food.

When they make food, they leave the oxygen behind. We use the leftover oxygen to breathe.

Algae (AL-jee) is a type
of protist you can see.

Some people call algae
pond scum. The algae
is food for some animals.

Do you see the frog?
It likes to eat algae.

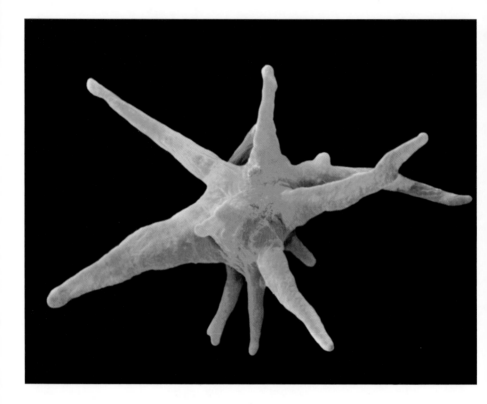

Amoebas (uh–MEE–buhs) live in puddles, too. They look like blobs. They move and eat by changing their shapes.

Amoebas eat other tiny life
in the puddle. This tiny
kind of life is a diatom
(DYE-uh-tawm).

21

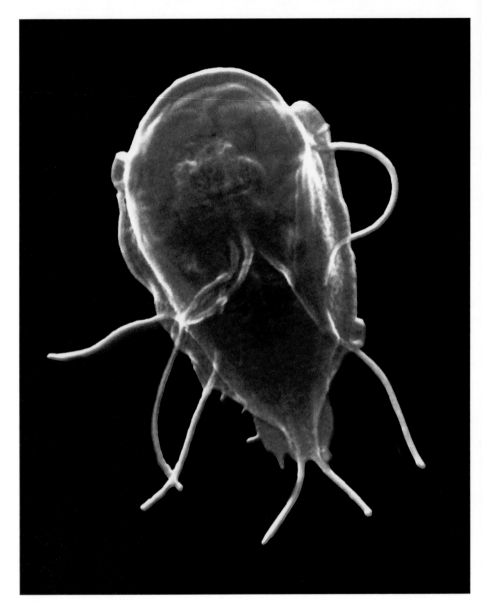

Some protists can make people sick.

This protist lives in unclean water. You will get a stomachache if you drink water that is not clean.

Bacteria (bak-TIHR-ee-uh) may also be in the puddle.

Bacteria is another kind of tiny life. Some bacteria can make you sick.

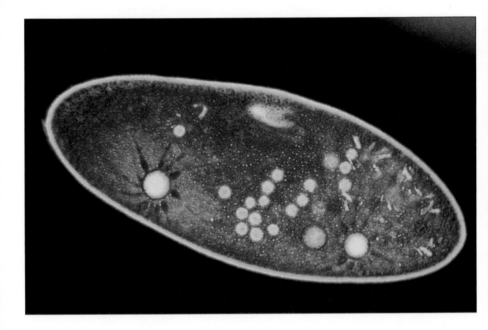

26

There is more tiny life in a puddle.

This one eats bacteria. It can eat up to 5,000 bacteria a day! Other kinds of tiny life may eat it, too.

Life in the puddle is very crowded.

You can't see the tiny life living there. But one drop of water can have more than 1 million kinds of tiny life.

29

Words You Know

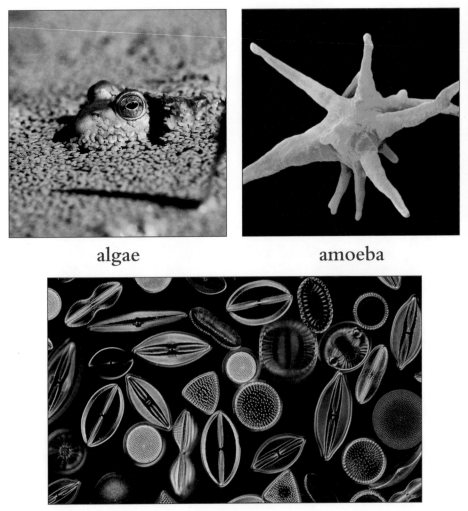

algae

amoeba

diatom

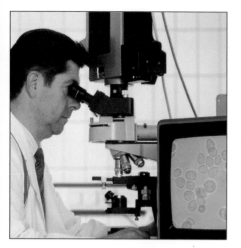

microscope

puddle

stomachache

Index

About the Author

Bobbi Early is a teacher and writer living in Kansas City, Missouri. She studied biology in college and still likes learning about animals of all sizes. This is her first book for children.

Photo Credits

Photographs © 2005: Bruce Coleman Inc./L.S. Stepanowicz: cover; Corbis Images: 9 (Lester V. Bergman), 5 (Cloud Hills Imaging Ltd.); Peter Arnold Inc.: 29 (Roland Birke), 21, 30 bottom (Darlyne A. Murawski); Photo Researchers, NY: 25, 31 bottom (Ken Cavanagh), 8, 26 (Eric V. Grave), 13 (SPL), 14 (Claire Ting); Phototake/Dennis Kunkel: 10; Stone/Getty Images/Michael Rosenfeld: 6, 31 top left; Superstock, Inc.: 3, 31 top right (Lisette Le Bon), 17, 30 top left; Visuals Unlimited: 18, 30 top right (Dr. Stanley Flegler), 22 (Dr. Fred Hossler).